L.O.V.E.
Lessons On Virtually Everything

A Collection of Words and Thoughts
Volume IV

L.O.V.E.
Lessons On Virtually Everything

A Collection of Words and Thoughts
Volume IV

Amber Whitted

Chicago

L.O.V.E. – LESSONS ON VIRTUALLY EVERYTHING: A COLLECTION OF WORDS AND THOUGHTS VOLUME 4

Copyright © 2021 by Amber Whitted. All rights reserved. Printed in the United States of America. No part of this book may be reproduced in any manner whatsoever without permission except in the case of brief quotations embodied in critical articles or reviews. Books by Eshe Words Literary Works may be purchased for educational, business, or sales promotional use.

www.amberwhitted.com

Cover artwork: Creative Blessings Design by Jelaine Bell, © 2021
Website: www.creativeblessingsdesign.com

Library of Congress Cataloging-in-Publication Data

Whitted, Amber, 1981 –
 – 1st ed p.cm
 ISBN-13: 978-0-578-96655-7
  1. Poetry 2. Poetry – African American 3. African American Literature I. Title

First edition: September 2021

10 9 8 7 6 5 4 3 2 1

"And now these three remain: faith, hope and love. But the greatest of these is *love*." (1 Corinthians 13:13)

Happy Birthday to me…

Table of Contents

Lessons Learned Along The Way

I: View From My Front Porch

Fight With Love	2
Immovable	6
Run	7
24	8
At The Core of It All	9
A Black History Lesson	10
Wildfires	11
Braggin'	12
Requested Narration	13
Supplication	14
2020 Recap	16

II: Everything He Needs To Know

If You Were Here	18
Example	23
Runnin'	24
Love Law #1	25
Terms and Conditions	26
That One Jill Song	30

Confessions	31
Serendipity	32
Intercessor	36

III: More Than One Meaning

Affirmations	40
Rise of the Pride	41
Hint	42
Say Goodbye	43
For Time	44
Fly	45
Finally	46
Two Feet	47
On Being Still	48
Trust the Process	49
To My Younger Self	50

IV: I'm Fine…and Other Lies I've Told

Scars	52
Baggage	53
Shrink	54
Dance Class	59
Natural	59

Me At 40	62
Homecoming	64
A Message to Wonder Woman	67
When A Woman Decides To Love Herself	68

V: She Follows the Light of the Sun

Light of the Sun	74
Until The Morning Comes	76
Seasons	77
Childish Faith	78
Surrender	82
Prayer	83
I Need You Now	84
For My Elders	84
No Holding Back	88
Breathe	89
Choose To Love	90
In The End	91

Lessons Learned Along The Way...

An introduction

Let the words of my mouth and the meditation of my heart be acceptable in your sight, O LORD, my rock and my redeemer. (Psalm 19:14)

Thank you, Father, for allowing me to have the gift of words and the chance to share them. I am grateful and humbled that You have chosen me. All glory and praise belong to You.

Growing up, I watched TV shows like "A Different World", "Living Single" and "Moesha". I tried to find myself in the characters and picture what my life would be like as I transitioned from high school to college and into adulthood. If you had asked me then, I would have told you that my friends and I would become extremely successful, have amazing families and dream jobs, and will remain close. We would be living life as if a camera was following us, waiting to insert a laugh track for moments of humor and sympathetic music for the times that we did shed tears – albeit few and far between. Yep, in my young mind, life would be perfect.

It wasn't though. Not one bit.

As time goes on, you learn that even your best-laid plans are subject to change. Not everyone who starts the journey with you makes it to the end. You understand that some roads are meant to be traveled alone. You begin to question everything that you knew to be true. Like everyone else, the time spent in quarantine helped me put my life into perspective and realize what was truly important.

It all came down to one word – Love.

Love is so much more than romantic relationships or the feeling we get when we "fall in love". It should be the root of all that we do. "Love always protects, always trusts, always hopes, always perseveres." (1 Corinthians 13:7). When given to self first, love can't help but flow into each life we touch.

The poems in this book are reflections of that love. They are things that I've seen, felt, and learned up to this point. It is my birthday gift to myself in celebration of how far I have come while acknowledging all that I have yet to see. My prayer is that you will feel the love on each page and be blessed by each word.

To all of those that I hold close to my heart – by blood or by bond, current or past, mentor or mentee: These words are for you. I know the love that you have for me will always be there. As long as I am able, I will show you how much I love you too.

If you never heard
those "three words" spoken to you,
know that *I love you.*

Be blessed, now and always!

L. O. V. E.
Lessons On Virtually Everything

A Collection of Words and Thoughts
Volume IV

I

The view from my front porch
is limited.
Still, I feel the souls
in each home not my own.

Fight With Love

Inspired by 1 Corinthians 13
These are the times we face...

Daily,
I watch as the souls of our sons
are sent to the slaughter.
I hear the tales of degradation
from the lips of our daughters.
Outside, I stay strong.
Inside, I cry tears,
wondering when it is enough.
Still,
you tell me to fight with love.

I see the disparity
in the education of our youth.
History tells them
that they were slaves and savages;
of their royalty, they have no clue.
I sit at the feet of the elders
and I pray to my God above.
All I am told is to fight with love.

But how?
How am I to fight with the one thing
that I'm not given?
How am I to believe that if I keep living
cycles will break
and all will be forgiven?
Being brown still means you're sinning,
and melanin murder is mass-produced.
Corporate dealings reinforce glass ceilings
and guns are the new noose.

Too many vigilantes are on the loose.
They hide behind badges
and ship kings in paddy wagons
to their new plantation,
leaving queens to raise a nation of children
alone.
Meanwhile, our elders are struggling
to keep the place that they call home.
They don't fit the need of modern greed,
so their homes are seized.
It seems that the dreams of King
have been delayed.
And despite what I see every day,
you want me to fight with love.

For some of this, I must blame us.
Wasn't there a time
when we could face each other
and respectfully nod?
Better yet, we would speak.
We could see the humanity
beyond familiarity
since it is the same goal
that we all seek –
respect.
Now, our race is a broken society
where the richest protect themselves
from their brother.
We classify ourselves
based upon skin color
and the texture of our hair,
making this the basis of our beauty.
Why is it no longer our duty
to reinforce purpose?

We don't talk to our youth,
but we call them uncouth
when they relate better to rap verses
that release curses
and drown out the voice of God.
The next generation finds it odd
to trust a being that they can't see,
so they thrive on strife
and take the very life that God gave.
Another body is placed in the grave
as tears are added to the crimson river
flowing through the streets.
I thought the goal was to find peace.
We're living on our knees
and you want me to fight with love.

Still,
love is patient –
patient enough to understand
that mankind needs to learn
to operate in compassion.
Love is kind –
kind enough to extend itself
when reciprocity is hard to find.
It does not envy,
it does not boast,
it is not proud.
Love never turns a blind eye
to the needs of those in the crowd.
It does not dishonor others,
is not self-seeking,
is not easily angered,
and records no wrongs.
Regardless of the hatred,

love seeks what's best for you
and keeps a humble song
free of evil and filled with truth.
It always protects,
always trusts,
always hopes,
and presses.
So my guess is that is why
love never fails.

Understanding all that love entails,
I wonder if I can swallow
what has been placed on my plate.
Love can be a heavy burden to bear,
but it is less to carry than hate.
I'll wait to receive
lessons from the Master.
I'll learn how to radiate hope
in the midst of disaster.
In the end,
maybe we'll find the freedom
that we've been dreaming of –
the day that we can stop fighting
and just love.

Immovable

We are like the souls before us –
united and unyielding,
powerful and peaceful,
fueled with faith and purpose.
We rise like the dawn.
We fear not the night.
We stand.
We fight.

Run

Run, boy, run!
Gotta run these streets.
Pick a pocket, pay no penance
'cuz your people gotta eat.
Trade what matters for money.
Have apathy and an alibi.
Shake the earth with every footstep
where a pool of blood resides.

Run, boy, run!
Accountability? No need.
A mother's tears are your legacy.
An ill-fated end is your planted seed.
The thing you fear is what you take.
Life lies in your hands.
It's time to stop running
and stand.

24

Every word,
thought
and action has weight.
Make tangible plans.
Please don't hesitate.
No time for fear.
Time won't last long.
24 hours…
gone.

At The Core of It All

A diminished hexaverse

Search for what is real.
Reach high and reach low.
Beg, borrow and steal
for something to feel
while trying to grow.

Deny the truth.
Perplex what's not.
Acting uncouth.
Muddle the plot.

Time reveals
facts that show
karma's view:

Always
has been

you.

A Black History Lesson

As kings and queens, you leered.
On boats in shackles, you cheered.
As slaves for purchase, you domineered.
Through it all, we persevered.

On paper freed, you jeered.
We built our own world; you interfered.
We rose again; you reappeared.
Through it all, we persevered.

We created; you commandeered.
We educated; you feared.
We made a name; you smeared.
Through it all, we persevered.

With our fists raised, you fleered.
With our families restored, you engineered.
Guns, drugs and broken homes – you sneered.
Through it all, we persevered.

While you plotted, we peered.
To failed justice, we still adhered.
Our full demise, we still veered.
Yes, through it all, we persevered.

Despite the fragments you profiteered,
the whole of our beauty has not yet appeared.
For everything we have pioneered –
through it all, we persevered.

Wildfires

May we always be inspired to inspire

Some wildfires cannot be contained.
They burn brightly in the souls
where they were placed.
Not encased,
but given a body to flourish.
Embers of art fly and nourish
those watching nearby,
granting permission
for their own flames to ignite
from complacent blues
to a passionate red.
Some wildfires cannot be contained.
They spread.

Braggin'

Marvelous melanin.
Talent trendsettin'.
Folks be forgettin'
the pace we be settin'.

We been on.
You ain't know?

Requested Narration

Based on a true story that we all saw on social media once or twice.

If you're going to tell our story,
tell the truth —
whole,
honest
and raw.
Show the versions you leave on social media
for us to awe at its gore.
Instead,
you scrub it on the editing floor.
You remove elements of gloom
and insert saviors that didn't exist.
The sting of honesty is dismissed
since the hero complex allows you
to remain in ignorant bliss.
You paint the picture
that you feel will sell more.
When what you see
doesn't pierce your core,
it's easier for you to digest.
But I humbly suggest
that if you're going to tell our story,
tell the truth —
not just the parts that serve you best.

Supplication

If you should find me with head bowed –
not raising fists or screaming out,
not showing rage or crying tears,
which is the sum of all your fears –
know that my eyes are still not dry.
I know my pleas have been denied.
Mercy is not equally shared.
The lives of my kin have not been spared.

If you should find me sitting still,
know I'm trying to follow His will.
I must sow peace while you wage war.
I must pour healing into each sore.
I must embody faith instead of fear.
I must show resolve when the way is unclear.
I must shine light in darkness' wake
and show what steps we all should take.

And if you find me, know my goal
is restoration of evil's toll,
so those that follow won't carry my plight
but walk in knowledge and in light.
The burden now passed on to me,
protested loud or on bended knee,
will increase in weight again
if we cannot bring it to end.

Still, I do not wish this alone.
One day, love will melt hearts of stone
and turn the tide to freely view
those of rich and darker hue.

So, if you find me with head bowed –
not raising fists or screaming out –
I pray not just for kin of mine,
I pray indeed for all mankind.

2020 Recap

an acrostic sonnet

We watched as media became gospel.
Hatred amongst brethren was commonplace.
Attempts to resolve were deemed as hostile.
Trust waned between the sexes and each race.
Disconnection grew; finances waivered.
Intellectuals banned against the poor.
Destitution plagued those deemed unfavored.
Weariness knocked on every human's door.
Everywhere you looked, there were tears shed; yet
light was still there for those who chose to see.
Each day we rose, we vowed not to forget
a better life begins with empathy.
Ready to move on and a new page turn,
now we must ask ourselves: What did we learn?

II

I struggle to be honest
about myself and how I feel.
I hope he'll be patient with me.
Within these lines are
everything he needs to know.

If You Were Here

I wanted to write about love.
I wanted to share my thoughts
about the innocent glances
given before warm greetings,
knowing that this was not happenstance.
I wanted to reminisce on the nervousness
that I heard in your voice
when you asked me my name,
and the humor in knowing
that your speech and my heartbeat
carried the same cadence.
You tried to be cool,
and I was a fool to believe
that you couldn't see my heart on my sleeve.
It had just been returned to me.
I pieced it together
with dreams and hope
and was too slow in returning it
to its proper place.

That was my fault.

I wanted to recall the words exchanged
during long distance conversations,
since the city was "so far away"
from the suburbs.
In your voice,
I heard the words of my next love poem
ringing in my ears.
Our talks penned lyrics to Duke.
In a Sentimental Mood,

you made me forget my Solitude.
And All Too Soon,
you had me wishing to be your Sophisticated Lady.

And baby, I wanted nothing more
than to write about that.

Remember that blue sweater I wore
on our first date?
Just so you know,
I changed clothes three times that night.
I wanted to make sure that
the impression was just right.
I tried to deny the butterflies,
but I was scared.
Love had arrived
and I wasn't prepared to tell you
that I had flaws.
You were so in awe of my natural beauty
that you didn't notice at all.
Infatuation made me overlook your scars.
Stars filled both of our eyes
and we fell in love before we knew
what we looked like in daylight.
In that moment, we were perfect.
So can you blame me
if I want to write about rainbows
and unicorns
and magic
and all the corny stuff
that made you sick?
Despite my overly optimistic view,
you would stick by me.
In your darkest hour,

I stuck by you.
I was the first call you made
and you always got through.

I wanted to write about that too.

I wanted to write about long drives
and deep sighs
and hand holding
and woven lives that turned into soul ties
because lies lay down next to truth
and changed the outcome
of what could've become a beautiful thing.
I gave my all; she got the ring.
It seems my time was in vain.
She's beautiful, by the way.
As much as I wish I could hate you,
I can't.
You placed the words of love on my lips
before your ship sailed for other shores.
I would have asked
why you don't want me anymore,
but I was afraid that I would not be able
to handle that spill.
It's a bitter pill,
and the sugar coating of knowing
how you will always feel
will not make it better.

I will pull myself together
to write about the naivety I lost
and the lessons I learned.
I'll cry over the walls I built
and the bridges I burned.

I'll pen limericks for the lemons that I ate,
straight with no chaser,
while you chased her.
With an eraser,
I'll remove any memories
of us that occurred.
Does she know that you loved me first?
Does she know that I formed the words
that you spoke to bring her near?
It was here that you learned
to make your feelings clear.
This poet posed as a ghostwriter,
teaching you the words needed
to make her stay.

And that is all I wanted,
for me anyway.

I'll take the words
that I didn't send with you
and use them to compose a soliloquy
that will eloquently explain my mistakes.
I'll write until I am rebuilt
and prepare for the one
who will fill that space.
I'll be patient,
no matter how long it takes.

Still, I can't help but wonder what if.
While I write scenarios in prose,
I know that it's in God's will
that I rest.
No matter what I may suggest,
even my most thorough explanations

would be no more than a feeble guess.
At best,
I will write about conversations,
blue sweaters,
first dates,
laughs,
loss and lessons.
All nostalgia,
but still blessings.

I will write about love,
even in your absence.

It would be the same
if you were here.

Example

I will show you how to love me
by loving myself.
If you can't duplicate,
I still will not lack
love.

Runnin'

a blues joint

My Mama told me that men will plan and boys will play.
You are just the type used to having things your way.
I can't get mad; you've never known accountability.
So, I'm thinking – maybe you should just go be free.
But you and I both know this is where you wanna be.

Everything about her is exactly what you desire.
I ignite your mind; she ignites your fire.
If you had to choose, you wanna go where you are pleased.
So, who am I to keep you from meeting all your needs?
But you and I both know this is where you wanna be.

I'm not the one to be chasing and misplacing my pride.
Maybe if you were ready, I would gladly put that aside.
Giving up the games is the place where you and I can't agree.
So, go ahead and live your life, but it won't be here with me.
And you and I both know this is where you wanna be.

But you keep on runnin', babe,
runnin' away from me.
Constantly runnin', babe,
from your destiny.
And you and I both know this is where you wanna be.

Love Law #1

No more pointless love poems.
No more statements of hopelessness
while hoping that love will guess
that you mean the opposite
and grant your heart's desire.
No more adding to the myth
that real love doesn't exist.
Truth is,
love starts
when you exhibit its definition.

Terms and Conditions

He said,
"For once,
I want you to be a bad girl.
The type I tell my friends
that it's the best I ever had kind of girl.
I want you to let go of all your inhibitions."

And I said,
Ok...
but that comes with terms and conditions.

I know that you're used
to dealing with women
that come with resumes.
They stay ready to drop down
as soon as you say so.
They go however low they need
to keep you.
That kind of drama,
is for willingly naive fools.
What I do is bring a selfless love
that makes you better,
prays you to your destiny
and helps you to apply pressure.
I'm warmth in bad weather.
Those before me, you'd easily forget her.
Everyone around you will notice the change
since we've been together.
But that change costs;
the best things in life aren't free.
It all starts with your decision

and proposal on one knee,
exchanging rings and things,
sealed with a kiss
and a lifetime guarantee.

Oh, I'm being bold?
Too picky?
I'm worth it.
Believe me.

My space is not available for rent or lease.
I refuse to have a list of tenants
that come and go as they please.
This temple is sacred.
I have no problem saying what I need.
But because I believe in reciprocity,
what I get I freely give.
Standing by your side,
we can build a Dynasty
so our children can follow their Passions
in this One Life To Live.
Yeah, that's the kind of stuff
you only see on TV.
We can act it out in reality,
if you're ready.

And yes,
I know I have yet to mention sex.
The thought of not answering your question
has you mildly perplexed
or even highly vexed.
My vagueness shouldn't come as a surprise.
Never forget –
luxury doesn't advertise.

This prize is heavenly,
that's why only one can win.
If you're interested,
truly interested,
I'll tell you where you can begin:
Master self
then talk to God about me.
He'll give you direction
on how to show affection
and speak my love language fluently.
That is true intimacy.
If you're into me, see Him.
I'm not one to live on a whim.
I'll remain patient
until God clearly shows
that you are "him".

And if you are the one
who holds the key,
then all the hugs
and the unconditional love
can come easily.
All the money skills in the daylight,
the touches you need at night,
the safe place to come home to,
and the love that you run to
can all be yours.
You can be as greedy as you like;
there will always be more –
if you can do what is necessary
to get in that front door.

Then,
and only then,

can I be your bad girl.
You won't tell your friends
but I'll be
"the best you ever had" kind of girl.
I'll be able to let go
and release my inhibitions
since you have met all
of my terms and conditions.

That One Jill Song

An acrostic

My mind wanders.
I wonder what you're doing now,
struggling with the curiosity
strong within my
innermost being.
Never mind though.
Good thing for me,
your photo and a favorite
old song is all I need to
undo the urge to call you.

Confessions

I am trying not to say it.
Once I do,
I officially give those feelings life.
I'd have to put away my pride,
cast my fears to the side,
and turn over what's inside
to your ego.
It's not that I don't trust you.
I just don't know
where this is meant to go.
This is nothing like what I'd expect,
and you never leave an overthinker
with too much time to reflect.
This felt too good to reject,
even though it was not
a part of my plan.
How can chaos and Kairos
go so beautifully hand-in-hand?
Please understand why I am trying
to maintain my tone.
I can't afford to be wrong
nor can I afford to sit here alone.
Once you say, "I love you",
those words are no longer your own.

Serendipity

Do you believe in fate?
I didn't, until I met you.
There were so many faces
in a crowded room,
but yours was the only one
to get through.
Before speaking, our souls knew
that connection was inevitable.
Never have I felt this level of déjà vu.
We both assumed
that someday we had crossed paths
or somewhere exchanged laughs.
In our past,
there had to be a link.
But in that moment our eyes met,
all we could think was
we were comfortable here.
Not one intention had been made clear,
but fear sat at bay long enough
to learn your name
as I timidly gave the same.

Should I blame kismet for this?
All logic was dismissed
as each conversation
pulled me closer to a dismissive
"It is what it is".
I can't operate that way.
I try to be meticulous
with each word that I say
as if I was a chess master,

or else this queen would get rooked
into a total disaster.
I can't afford to lose games right now.
You made me believe
that our closeness was ok.
I took the risk to play
as I began to trust
everything you'd say.
I allowed myself
to become less cynical.
My heart became open,
and with minimal thought,
I allowed my walls to come down –
still unsure if this would endure
or if you would stick around.

Was this no more than chance?
Each moment we spent
danced in my head
to a tune resembling
soul music on a Saturday night.
We were warm,
beautiful,
and smooth.
I provided the lyrics;
you provided the tune.
The back of my mind screamed,
"Too soon!"
and that I should know better.
This bond hadn't been tested
against stormy weather.
I was too infatuated,
feeling light as a feather.
I allowed myself

to be caught in your air,
fully aware that water
can safely reside there
but eventually must come back down
to earth.
And that is where it hurts.
For what it's worth,
we did our best to cushion the blow
and protect each other's hearts
as we tried to let go.

Still, I know that this was destiny.
It was no accident that time and space
brought you to me.
You held a mirror to my soul
to remind me it was beautiful,
and I showed you that you were loved
unconditionally.
While we know that some things are best
if they are left to just be
without pressure or rush
and with intentionally,
we know this cannot be dismissed.
So, consider this my admission.
Without permission,
I'm willing to say that
you changed me for the better.
God knows what we need
and how we'll heed,
and I believe
that you fulfilled His mission.
I pray I did the same for you.
I hope that I provided light,
peace,

and abundance of truth
as I was supposed to
and will do
as long as time allows.
When stars are meant to align,
they always cross paths somehow.

Intercessor

For my husband, written in the middle of the night

I pray for you without ceasing
because that is what the Word says to do.
I bombard heaven with my thankfulness for us
and I don't even know you –
but my spirit does.
It feels you
seeking and praying for me.
The least that I can be
is found ready,
waiting in the place
where God will have us meet.

I know you exist.
In my mind, I've kissed your lips
and offered sweet encouragement
for your endeavors.
I've already gotten upset
about your truthfulness
when you were only trying
to make me better.
So even though we are not
physically together,
I will humbly serve as your intercessor.
I'll be found boldly going
to the throne of grace on your behalf.
I don't have to know where you're at
to know your need.
Without fear,
I'll plead for relief of whatever ails you,
from the thorn in your side

to your ego and pride.
I'll be here,
going into detail on how I wish
for our God to keep you safe,
to keep you humble,
and to make your name great amongst kings.
From the outside looking in,
these seem like silly things
to pray for a man
that has not made himself known.
But if I say that I love you,
how can I let you pray alone?

I know the Father hears my words
and sees the tears that I cry for you.
We will meet when the season is due,
and the manifestation of all my prayers
will come true.
Until then, I will practice my selflessness
by praying for a man
that I haven't even met.
This will be done without pause or regret.
I will gladly rise
whenever the Spirit presses,
because my guess is
that is when you need me the most.
I will join in chorus
with the heavenly host
so my worship becomes a weapon,
fighting against all attacks of the enemy
on your purpose,
goals and dreams.
I'll be up for hours,
praying that you receive power

to push past limits
that you thought existed.
I'll ask God to grant mercy
if He showed you the mark
and you missed it.

I won't quit
when we are finally face to face.
Even when we embrace,
I know it will be reason
to pray for you more.
I'll request to be your peace
and help to restore the balance
that this cold world tries to steal.
Daily, I'll ask that He helps you to heal
as He give me ways to show you
that my love is real.
And this love will be spoken
in the language that you understand –
without pretense or demand.

But until I am blessed to hold your hand,
I will pray for you without ceasing
because that is what the Word says to do.
My faith knows
that my words are getting through.
I'll wait prayerfully
until I see you.

III

Sometimes,
the words have more
than one meaning.

(acrostic poems)

Affirmations

All of me –
falls and rises,
fear and faith –
is more than capable of
running this race.
Marching forward is no longer
an option, but a mandate.
This moment in time
is a dedicated date for
open-armed receipt of all the
new blessings meant for this
soul.

Rise of the Pride

It's more than a hashtag

Believe me when I tell you that
lions do rise.
At the appointed time, we hear the
call to action and
kingdoms do fall.
Latency ends as
instructions are given to
vanquish the reign of
ego and arrogance.
Somehow, you missed it before.
Maybe then, it will make sense.
All this time, you desperately
tried to keep us docile by
telling us that our emotions were hostile.
Every time, however, lions still
rise.

Hint

Here's that clue that you're missing. Internalize and be willing to listen. Now is your chance to grow up and take your "L" gracefully.

Say Goodbye

Sometimes the hardest things
are the most necessary.
Yesterday is short-lived, and
gone is the chance to
overturn decisions made.
Open hearts played hands, now time
demands that the game must end.
Be grateful for the moments spent.
You have more to see beyond this
etched memory.

For Time

This go-around,
I'll focus on
my dream before
"eventually" becomes "never".

Fly

Freedom comes after the leap.
Lose your fear long enough to allow
yourself to soar.

Finally

Freedom came
in just one moment.
Not with labored effort or
additional tears; by
lifting the veil of fear, peace gladly
lent an ear when she said
"Yes" to herself.

Two Feet

Too many times, I've been burned
without adequate warning
or intelligent reason.
Friends be scandalous, they say.
Everyone that claims to love, doesn't.
Everyone that claims to speak truth, won't.
This time, I'll stand on my own.

On Being Still

Before you speak too hastily,
ending what could and just might be:
Stop. Fall back for just a bit.
Take a moment to simply sit.
Internalize all that you feel.
Leverage silence to help you heal.
Lessons, in time, will be revealed.

Trust the Process

The journey isn't easy.
Rises and falls frequent the
undertaking that you pursue.
Sometimes you will doubt
the calling given to you and
this is what "they" wish.
Hear me on this:
Every step gets you closer.
Press on, even with little to give.
Rest, but never cease to live.
Open your mind to change.
Clear your heart of hurt.
Each day brings confirmation
so you'll always know your worth.
Stay your course, and never forget to…

To My Younger Self

It's time

I owe you.
The dreams you had
still stay with me and
take residence in my mind.
If you still wish to
make magic and fly, then bruised
ego aside, I will try.

IV

I'm fine...

...and other lies I've told.

Scars

It's time to let it go

Some scars don't heal.
They're always ready to bleed.
They're constant reminders
of the cuts that we received
after warnings we didn't heed.
They encourage more tears.
They embrace our doubts
and enable our fears.

Some scars don't heal.
They leave us wondering why
the memory won't leave
or the pain won't subside.
When will we,
after the complaints and groans,
learn to just leave them
alone?

Baggage

I haven't been honest with you.
There are places that I refuse
to let anyone into.
Since you choose
to see the beautiful parts of me,
that is what I make readily available
for you to see.
But honestly, I'm broken.
I'm damaged.
I carry plenty of baggage,
things that I need to let go of,
and ugly bad habits.
The truth is I'm scared.
If I let you see that side of me,
I'm not prepared to let you go.
You've nourished parts of me
that I thought were dead;
you've helped me to grow.
I don't think you understand
how integral that is
to a soul like mine.
People like you are rare gems,
you're hard to find.
It's gonna take some time
to undo this mess that was made.
You said this was unconditional.
All that I can do is pray
that if I let you fully in,
you'll stay.

Shrink

As a woman,
this world feels better when you shrink.
When the size of your frame
isn't comfortably tamed,
you can be easily blamed
for any disdain people have for you.
Every laugh and insult
that they throw is earned
since you haven't learned
to maintain an acceptable figure.
You're just not pretty when you're bigger.
Starvation becomes your friend.
Again and again,
you deprive yourself of any joy you can have
with the feeling that
beauty lies on the other end.
And this becomes your goal.
Nevermind the emotional toll,
the mental hold,
or the spiritual hole you fall in.
For physical approval, you're all in
to the point where you have the gall
to ignore your own needs.
How important is it truly to please?

As a woman,
this world feels better when you shrink.
When your ambition is too large,
they find it hard to accept you as a lady.
Any move you make is deemed
as emasculating or shady.

You're always evaluating every vision
that God gave you.
How could truth be there
if no one else cares?
The idea of a woman with a plan
is too much to bear.
In the interest of being fair,
you downplay your role.
You allow your ideas to be stolen
to get a seat at the table.
Your thoughts of progression
become no more than a fable
and you begin to believe
that you're no longer able.

As a woman,
this world feels better when you shrink.
When you have the audacity to speak,
folks wonder if your brain and mouth
are in sync.
No one cares what you think,
or at least that is what you are told.
They say,
"You're too lovely to be loquacious.
Silence is golden."
You become sold on self-censure,
because a lady is seen and not heard.
The idea of more
than your beauty mattering
becomes absurd.
It's a man's world,
and you were only made to serve.
Nevermind those words
welling up in your belly,

it's more important to be viewed
as pretty rather than petty.

So we listened.
So I listened.

Every time I allowed myself to shrink,
a piece of my spirit died.
I tried to drown out the cries
with makeup and heels.
I covered my feelings with a smile
and a softly spoken, "It's alright."
I exuded happiness throughout the day
and hated my reflection at night.
The fight in me died.
Self-care became a luxury
that I couldn't afford.
I started taking notes
from so-called experts
on how to be better adored
until the core of me
could barely be restored.
Was it worth it
if I no longer saw me anymore?

It's not.
What is so important about aesthetics
that it made me forget
all the things about me
that are unique?
They are visible with my presence
before I even speak.
All I have to do is breathe
and those around me believe

that I was born for greater.
I had to get to a point
Where pushing my purpose for later
was no longer an option.
I stopped sipping the toxin that told me
that my talent and ability,
combined with ingenuity,
was killing my femininity.
How could that be
if the very God that created these curves
made them to house unlimited possibility?

So, this is me.
I've done the work
to heal the hurt
and improve my state of mind.
Not everyone is worthy of my essence,
my wisdom,
my touch
or my time.
I will carry myself
as a woman in high demand.
If this is too much for you,
I understand,
but I will not apologize.
I will not take my eyes off my prize.
I'll still root for you
but not at the expense of my soul.
Call me cocky.
Call me brash.
Call me arrogant.
Call me bold.
Whatever boosts your ego
is not my concern.

I'm certain that this direction
is one that I have earned.
Through falling, I've learned.
Through self-love, I've gotten up,
dusted myself off,
filled my own cup
and made the changes to secure
my physical and spiritual wealth.

Allow me to reintroduce myself.
I'm a woman
no longer interested in shrinking
because it is bad for my health.

Dance Class

I was told that fat girls
can't wear tights
or leotards
or ballet shoes.

We can't wear costumes
or sequins
or buns
or red lipstick.

Fat girls can't be on stages
in recitals
under tricolor lights
or soft spots.

No solos.
If we gotta be there,
put us in the corner
in the back row
so no one can see the tutu
digging into our fat rolls.

I was told that fat girls
can't wear tights.

Guess I didn't know.
I was too busy
dancing to the rhythm
in my soles.

Natural

I'll always remember the day
that I decided to stop living the lye.
For years, I tried to hide.
Deep inside,
I searched to find my natural truth.
I admired photos of women
with their crowns,
donning their glory
in such a regal way.
I longed for the day
where I could be free to join them.
Dynamic
Natural
Afros
know their history
and pass down the legacy
through thick, coily tresses.
Their voices beckoned me
beyond the need
to be socially acceptable and tamed.

Then one night, I was ready
for my crown to be reclaimed.

I slowly touched the curls
hidden beneath straightened strands.
They begged,
no,
demanded to be seen
for who they were.
Black Girl Magic, undefined.

Free.
Mine.
With scissors in hand,
I watched my hair fall to the floor.
Processed no more,
fear filled my heart
as I wondered what was now to be.
Staring back at me
was raw, imperfect beauty.
I owed myself to love this woman
for whom she was.
She waited too long to be seen.
Now, it was her time.

Me At 40

Inspired by the painting "Puffs and Paradise"
by Just A Girl With A Brush

I'm not the woman that I used to be.
Many things within me have changed.
I've learned to take responsibility
where I once placed blame.
My aura is tame.
I've learned to think before I speak,
not out of fear of being perceived as weak
but rather wise.
Light once lost has returned to my eyes,
and they are firmly fixated on the prize.
I'm no longer afraid
of taking some journeys alone.
There are some things
best done on your own.
If I need help,
I've learned to pick up the phone.
My idea of a good time
has changed from going out
to a good chill.
Music moves me –
always has, always will.
My rhythm still is questionable,
and droppin' it like it's hot
has turned into
setting it down like it's lukewarm.
I sleep better through thunderstorms.
I know the reason that I was born
is not contingent upon man's word.
I find shrinking absurd
unless we are discussing my waistline.

Even then, I still find time
for a good brownie or burrito.
My ego has lowered.
Most of my pride has been released.
Self-care is no longer a luxury.
I am determined to keep my peace
at all costs.
I don't have to be the boss,
but you will respect me.
I will fight for your cause,
but I cannot neglect me.
Ultimately, I must be satisfied
with the version of me
that I lay with each night.
I've exhausted the will to fight
with one committed
to always being right.
If what I say won't sway you,
then I won't bother.
I refuse to give you fodder
to feed the foolishness
that you wish to maintain.
I'm no longer obligated
to carry your baggage or pain
unless I choose to.
I know a lot of this may confuse you.
But this is me at 40.
I've grown a lot.
I still have more growing to do.

Homecoming

What happens when worlds collide

Slowly,
I'm being reminded
of everything that I let go.
I'm returning to the soul that I was
before I released her
in the name of compromise.
My eyes have been reopened
and I don't know
if they can close again.

I'm remembering
the things that made me whole.
They were all placed there
by a God who knew
I'd know what to do with them.
Gifts given to be shared,
not to be compared with others
as if they were the same.
I was reminded
of my place in the game,
born to embrace the race
not meant to be run by anyone else.

But to keep the peace,
I released pieces of myself
with the hope that
the sacrifice would be appreciated.
The dream of being one with one
was renegotiated too many times
and the original premise was lost.

I was left to wonder
if it was worth the cost.

One day, I crossed paths
with my own reflection.
I sat still long enough to hear
my original direction
call me by name.
Inspiration called to reclaim
the daughter who tried to run
from home.
Sweetly,
softly,
not judging my choice to roam.
Instead,
it whispered who I was meant to be,
reassurance that destiny
always finds you somehow.
God works like that.
He moves on your spirit
and uses faith to reinforce fact.

And that is where I stand.
I'm at a crossroad,
knowing that the choice I make
may cost me
what I've tried to build.
Still,
I'm being reminded
of everything that I let go.
I'm returning to the soul that I was
before I released her
in the name of compromise.
My eyes have been reopened

and I don't know
if they can close again.

A Message to Wonder Woman

I wonder why we women
always try to be wonder women,
then wonder when we get weak
who is coming to save us.
The same ones that we cape for
end up putting us to the side.
Out of pride,
we tie our cape even tighter.
Sis,
who told you that you always
have to be a fighter?
Relax sometimes.
Settle into your beauty.
Take that "S" off your chest.
It ain't always your duty
to save everyone.
Make sure that your spirit is full.
Now,
wouldn't that be wonderful?

When A Woman Decides To Love Herself

When a woman doubts herself,
the world celebrates.
Every time she berates
her God-given features,
her haters hear her loud and clear,
echoing her sentiment.
Every word spoken to her detriment
is heaven-sent to hell-raisers.
They won't raise her esteem,
but they will make memes
that crush dreams
and rip souls at seams.
It seems that she should know better,
but her endeavor for love
has her settling for likes.
She'll hike up her skirt,
throw on music to twerk,
and use makeup to mask the hurt.
She knows she needs to heal,
but she gon' do it for the 'gram first.

When a woman doubts herself,
she doesn't see her value.
She consumes foolishness in volume
and assumes that someone
will come to her with the opposite.
She's desperate for comfort.
Instead, she gets wrapped up
in fifteen seconds of fame
and a lifetime of regret.
She wanted confirmation;

all she got was degradation.
She craved real intimacy;
all she got was sex,
a soul tie to collect,
and he's on to the next.
She reflects,
but not long enough to deal.
She knows she needs to heal,
but tweets fly high and reveal all.

She forgets everything about her
that is divine.
She dims her own light
because how dare she shine
when her flaws are showing.
If she opens her mouth,
everyone will know her business
and this is her biggest fear.
So she stays behind a keyboard,
getting on one accord
with those who only want
to cut and kill.
She knows no one is exempt;
still, she hopes it is God's will
that her time never comes.
If it does,
her self-deprecation and low valuation
will cause her to be undone.

But,
when she decides to look in the mirror,
really look in the mirror,
she'll notice the natural beauty
that Mac can't make.

She'll stop curving her curves
and embrace those hips that
cause the foundations
of the earth to shake.
She'll begin to take chances,
learning that her first romance
must be with herself.
Without permission from anyone else,
she'll strip her insecurities
one by one.
She'll loose everything unfair,
remove everything she can't bear,
until it's only her standing there –
bare before her Heavenly Father
with nothing to offer
but her soul.
And at that moment when she
lets God take control,
self-esteem takes ahold
and she knows who she is.

She realizes that her imperfections
are a direct reflection
of a God of perfection
and made to His specifications.
Her design was no accident,
despite what her parents did.
She births nations
even if she never births a kid.
She's crowning while crowning
the leaders of the next generation,
but she doesn't neglect
her own preparation.
Blessings flow to her gravitationally.

She works a room graciously.
If something is a waste of her time,
she exits gracefully.

With open hands, she receives love.
With open heart,
she gives love without fear,
despite what the world does.
She's released unrealistic expectations
of those in her life.
She celebrates herself
in lace and diamonds
even without being a wife.
She basks in God's light.
Her melanin soaks in determination,
dreams
and destiny.
It's impossible for her
to have a deficiency
since the Son gave this flower
all the vitamins that she needs.
She believes in what she sees,
has put to rest what's already done,
and has the faith to perceive
what has yet to come.
When each night is done,
she ends it with gratitude
so her attitude raises her aptitude.
Nothing you say or do
can spoil her mood.

When a woman decides to love herself,
her spirit rejoices,
for this is the one thing

it has wanted for so long.
Even in those moments
where she may not be strong,
she remembers that she is still worthy
and holds on to that pride.
Despite what the world may bring
or the tears that she's cried,
every morning she'll rise
and face herself to say,
"Good morning, Beautiful.
I love you."

V

She follows the light of the sun,
for darkness can't hide
from the ray of light given to her
by her Father.

Light of the Sun

How this "sunflower" tries to live each day

If you seek me, you'll find me easily.
I'm the one stretched high
for the world to see.
Not for their eyes,
but for what I need.
I crave the light of the sun.
Every morning,
to the east I face,
patiently waiting for You
to grace my world.
And I smile wholeheartedly.
I open intentionally
so not one part of me misses
the blessings You provide so freely.
Willingly, I spend my days
turning to stay face to face
with the One who shows me the way.

When my earth fell flat,
You kept me grounded.
You molded my sphere of influence
so I'd be well-rounded.
You planted my roots
firmly in the earth.
As the rains came,
they nourished me just the same.
You said,
"Let her grow as a testament
to what My Love and Light can do."
When I struggled to see You,

You parted the clouds
for just enough light to get through
and I still bloomed.
Not even the darkness
could prevent Your truth.
How beautiful I must be to You!

I'll follow the light,
wherever it may lead.
If I take heed to Your Word,
You promised to birth
something new in me.
There'd be life abundantly given,
which is my right as an heir.
Favor ain't fair,
so I never take for granted
each chance I receive
to bask in Your rays.
With my roots anchored
in Your peace,
I'll release the dirt that tried
to hold me down.
I'll lift high the petals
that You gave me
to wear as my crown.
I'll gladly embrace Your warmth,
standing in reverence and awe.
Here, my beauty is exposed.
Here, I give honor to my God.

Until the Morning Comes

I was raised to believe
that the dawn always comes
after the darkest night.
Even when fear has reached its height,
light comes in and brings new life abundantly,
just like God's Word said it would be.
Please push past thoughts of negativity
and really hear me.
There are things that we'll never understand,
but every plight and problem
are all a part of God's plan.
They are a perfect paradox
pieced together in divine order,
ready to move this world forward
and benefit the sons and daughters
walking according to His purpose.
I know you're used to hearing worthless curses,
but I'm here to tell you what your worth is
through positivity and verses.
Now the choice is yours.
You can relinquish your peace,
or you can rest in your power.
You can cry all night,
or you can sing through the midnight hour.
Even when the sun has hidden her face away,
the stars know exactly which notes to play.
They'll keep you in your joy,
keep you from being undone,
and give you the comfort that you need
until the morning comes.

Seasons

Snow covers the ground beneath
then melts to nourish flowers in spring.
Rain falls to earth to cool summer's heat
and paves the way for autumn leaves.
So do our days progress with time –
giving lessons to grow the mind
and show all that we have to gain
as life goes on and seasons change.

Childish Faith

I be approaching God
with my hands out
but never with my hands up
in surrender or release.
Always ready to receive,
I be begging God,
"Please, give me...
bless me...
increase my..."
Nevermind the obedience required.
I only seek what I desire,
inspired by the glimpses
of the lives
on my computer screen.
I be thinking their grass
is always green,
never seeing the tears
that water their lawn.

I be going on and on
about how I want God
to change other people,
as if the issue ain't right here.
I stay pointing fingers
when the problem is clear.
I be thinking
that fixing folk will work
without having to work out
my own insecurities.
I be asking God
to deal with everyone

but me.

I treat God like a genie –
grant me my wish then disappear
until I need You again.
I be questioning
why I can't feel His Presence
like I wasn't the one
that bottled Him up,
only rubbing out some prayers
when I am at my least.
I be wanting elevation
while forgetting
that we are called to be decreased.
I was told to have childlike faith,
one that trusts the Father
and obeys when asked.
This ain't that.
This be that childish faith.
It's greedy and easy to break.
It only goes to God
for what it can get
and to fix my mistakes.
But when it comes time
to submit to His will,
I don't have what it takes.
Or do I?
Am I humble enough to try,
or am I too filled with pride
to be clear on the real reason
my prayer was denied?

This be the side of the saints
that they sweep under the rug.

We all have had that moment
where our concern is short-sighted,
selfish,
and not Christ-minded.
Then we get humbled.
We get cut.
We bleed.
We out here looking
for that little mustard seed,
thinking that will appease God.
We know that we can do better.
Still,
He's ready and willing
to get us together
once we've weathered seas
that we were never meant to sail.
When we try to abandon ship,
He sends a whale.
He listens to each wail and moan
until we come to our senses
and leave our childishness alone.

I be wondering what God sees in me.
How does He see so much potential
in such a plagued body?
How does He see a stunning canvas
despite the errors splattered around?
How can He hear a beautiful melody
in the painful sound of my cries?
I be wanting to figure it out,
but I couldn't if I tried.
And that is why
I could never be God
in effort or mind.

I guess it's time to put
my childish ways
behind.

Surrender

At my weakest moment,
I fell to my knees,
surrendered,
and found my strength.

Prayer

If strength is found in standing,
power is found in prayer.
Kneeling's humility removes demanding
and God will meet us there.
Hard times notwithstanding,
our lives are eased with loving care
into our solution's landing
and our soul's needed repair.

I Need You Now

Inspired by the song by Smokie Norful

Lord, I need you without delay.
I know some seasoned saints
will warn me to watch what I say,
but I feel myself wasting away.
Have You forgotten me?
Left me to my own devices
and abandoned me?
Or has the sin
that I've wrapped myself in
made You feel
as if You can't stand me?
So candidly, I'm speaking.
I'm drowning slowly
in my own tears
and my ship is sinking.
My story wasn't supposed
to be like this.
I promised to follow You
in whatever it is.
It started off as bliss,
until my frailties failed me
and I fell through a trap door.
Now, I can't see You anymore.
My vision is vailed by vanity.
I keep doing the same things
to pull myself out –
the definition of insanity.
Can it be any clearer
that I can't fix this?
It is something

that only You can handle,
and nothing that I can scramble
can get me out of this place.

To be honest,
I'm losing that mustard seed of faith
that I had in You.
I thought that if worked hard enough,
I'd eventually push through.
My ideas were fool proof.
I wrote the vision and made it plain.
I thought that if I threw in
some scriptures and shouting,
I'd have heaven to gain.
I dressed myself in my own pride,
crossed into Your lane,
and feigned interest in Your plans.
I called my self-righteousness holiness
and never asked You where I truly stand.
So should I have been shocked
when You required that I stand down?
My best laid plans turned into a circus
and I was the main clown.
My so-called friends stood around
to watch my demise.
No one willing to empathize
but were ready to capitalize on my fall.
Surprise!
I can't do it all.
Now, it's to You that I call.

I'm supposed to have victory,
but I don't see that outcome.
This is a race that You said

You'd prepare me for,
but I feel outrun.
Not one part of me feels
that I've begun that ascent.
I'm tired,
I'm frustrated,
I'm lonely,
and I'm spent.
All those times I moved without You,
I know I should have waited.
I can only pray
that my blessings are not negated.
Because God, I need you.
I'm reaching for You
despite being covered
by the spots of my sins.
Just me,
minus the nine,
praying You don't care where I've been.
I need healing and direction.
I no longer want to be proud.
If I can't touch Your hand,
then I'll crawl through a crowd.
And if I can't move,
then I pray someone will lift me up
to lay me at Your feet.
All I ask, Son of David,
is that You have mercy on me.
Whatever it is You require,
that I will be.
I don't need anything else.
It's You that I need.

For My Elders

Thank you for giving, teaching and loving

My hands are wrinkled.
My soul is weary.
I got ways to go,
though my body is tired.
The race isn't won
and needs me to fight.
I got ways to go
through water and fire.
Too many others want me.
Too many others need me.
Too many others rely
on my spirit to inspire.
And I got ways to go,
so many ways to go,
before I retire.

No Holding Back

For the SRBL family

Why do you keep holding yourself back?
You're probably waiting
for someone to save you,
but the Savior has already given you
everything that you needed
and that is a fact.
But you keep looking
to this and that
and it's throwing you out of whack.
Just take a step back.
Remember everything that you've created.
When it comes to your purpose,
it will no longer be debated.
You'll be elated to know
that the Father still expects greatness,
has factored in your fear,
and even forgiven your lateness.
Honestly,
you're still right on time.
Every one of your falls and rises
have been aligned in the divine.
Get out of that mindset
that there's something that you lack.
Stop holding yourself back.

Breathe

Breathe.
Inhale.
Exhale.
Release the rush
the world places on you.
No one told you
to take that weight upon you.
It's not mandatory.

Breathe.
Inhale.
Exhale.
Push through the pressure
and find your peace.
Reclaim your joy by any means.
Happiness is fleeting.
Joy is an internal contentment
that outlasts pain's meaning.

That is why you're still breathing.

So,
breathe.

Choose to Love

I still choose to love,
even as this world appears
to fall apart.
I'm still responsible
for this beating heart
and it chooses to love.
I choose to speak life
into your being,
dropping the seeds of positivity
that you need to bloom
into something beautiful.
Of hurt and pain,
this world is full,
but I still choose to love.
And as I gift this gift,
I only ask one thing:
With every fiber of your being,
allow this ember to turn into a flame.
Despite every person's race or creed,
call them by name
and let them know
that they are loved.
Still choose,
like I choose,
to love.

In the End

When all has been said

Take the risk,
but use discernment.
Failure is not the end,
it's an invitation to start again.
Never forget your worth.
Walking alone is ok.
Yes, this thing called life will hurt.
You will question.
You will cry.
But you will also laugh
and dance
and sing
and write
and pray
and heal
and grow
and learn
and live
and love.

That's all I have so far.
Honestly,
that's all you need to know.

www.ingramcontent.com/pod-product-compliance
Lightning Source LLC
Chambersburg PA
CBHW030223170426
43194CB00007BA/844